THE VILLAGE COQUETTE

Borgo Press Books by CHARLES DUFRESNY

The Spirit of Contradiction & The Double Widowing: Two Plays
Straight from the Convent & The Interrupted Wedding: Two Plays (with Florent Dancourt)
The Village Coquette & The Crazy Wager: Two Plays (with Florent Dancourt)

THE VILLAGE COQUETTE & THE CRAZY WAGER

TWO PLAYS

CHARLES DUFRESNY

With Florent Dancourt;
Translated and Adapted by Frank J. Morlock

THE BORGO PRESS
MMXIII

THE VILLAGE COQUETTE & THE CRAZY WAGER

Copyright © 1986, 2000, 2013 by Frank J. Morlock

FIRST EDITION

Published by Wildside Press LLC

www.wildsidebooks.com

For Jannet

CONTENTS

THE VILLAGE COQUETTE; OR, THE SUPPOSED LOTTERY 9
CAST OF CHARACTERS 11
ACT I 13
ACT II 41
ACT III 77
THE CRAZY WAGER, with Florent Dancourt . 97
CAST OF CHARACTERS 99
THE PLAY 101
ABOUT THE TRANSLATOR 181

THE VILLAGE COQUETTE; OR, THE SUPPOSED LOTTERY

CAST OF CHARACTERS

The Baron

The Widow, his neighbor

Argon, another neighbor

Girard

Lucas, farmer

Lisette, the coquette

ACT I

Girard (holding two letters and reading them)

From Paris. To Monsieur Le Baron of Hamlet. Let's take care of this letter for him. He's not at home. (putting the Baron's letter in his pocket, he opens the other letter) And the other's for me, Girard. I dare to hope that the list of winning lottery numbers is in this letter. Right, my cousin, the master printer in Paris, favors the role I've taken. Love is my guide in this roguery. With this false lottery list I am going to obtain Lucas' daughter as my wife.

Widow (entering)

I am waiting for Mr. Argon. Why hasn't he come?

Girard (reading the letter)

From Paris. "My dear cousin, before having distributed the list of lottery winners, I've sent you a false list, as you asked me to do, so you can have a big joke in your village. You can make your rival believe that Farmer Lucas won the grand prize of one hundred thousand francs." With this, I hope to obtain my Lisette. Lucas, believing his fortune made, will cede me his lease on the farm. He's the type to be caught in such a snare. At bottom, it's for his own good. By making me his son-in-law, he can't lose. (to Widow) But, why are you standing around dreaming?

Widow

Because Mr. Argon is supposed to come find me.

Girard

He'll be here soon. He's still in the château.

Widow

I'm getting impatient.

Girard

What for? You're not excited by a tender love. It's an old lover, and you should wait without impatience, coldly.

Widow

Shut up, Girard. Shut up. You know how I value him.

Girard

To believe an old man is an old greybeard is no big crime. I honor him more, being his collector. The collection is small and for you, with all my heart, I wish I could pay him one hundred thousand francs of income.

Widow

That would be too much for me, a former maid. That's what I was when I was in Paris. But here I have a higher rank, which I obtained from my late husband, a head magistrate. Thus, I've been ennobled in this village, a fine nobility at bottom, and which is worth a good bit, a nobility that one can take to Paris.

Girard

Let's renew our discussion and talk of Lisette again. Because, having so much power over her, being her neighbor, and a sort of surrogate parent, you are working hard to turn her into a coquette, instead of making her wiser.

Widow

Language of Paris. That's what will make her perfect.

Girard

Some perfection! Alas, you make her worse, when you come here to refine her wit. You make her heart more false and more vain.

Widow

At nine years, she was already a coquette in embryo. I have only pointed her in her natural direction—so her beauty will not prove worthless and she will profit by a fine marriage. I only want Lisette to be wise. She's naturally exquisite, and I've simply added to her talents all that I have learned.

Girard

With so many perfections, you will make her a prodigy of coquetry.

Widow

So much the better, I tell you. That's what makes beauty and wit valued. We've argued about this so many times. By coquette I mean a girl who is very wise, who knows how to take advantage of other's foibles, who always exhibits sang-froid in the midst of dangers, one who profits from opportunity which she knows how to manage, and uses her reason when we lose ours. A wise coquette is more knowing than anyone else because she is always exposed and always in a battle. One cannot deny that the strongest virtue is one that undergoes and survives the hardest tests. The coquette has prerogatives much more beautiful than a prude's. That beautiful right is the right of being happy. A prude, in her life, marries but once or twice, but the clever coquette never marries at all. She flatters, she raises hopes, she promises, but she never gives in—thus through her wisdom leaving each one to his love and desires, she makes pleasure last.

Girard

In my opinion Lisette is making my pain too harsh. It's useless to complain to her father, alas, complaining is no good. He scorns me.

Widow

Yes, because you are leaving your condition in life. You are soliciting my relative and you are only a flatfoot.

Girard

Very flat-footed, right. But, without belittling myself. Do I owe Lucas respect? He owes me some, perhaps. But now each of us rests on his pedestal, and for a collector to be the son-in-law of a farmer, it's by right of the game.

Widow

Good. It's an old game. Regretfully, I see your scheme is in ruins. Lisette repents of having considered you, and she says she no longer intends to have Girard. Now, the proud father and daughter find that your fortune is too recent. Everywhere you find ungrateful hearts, as in the village, even with regrets. But, during sometimes, gamble, pilfer, respect, trim, clip, loot and loot again. By force of conceit, you will come to listen.

Girard

Today my love appears bold to you, you blame my scheme. Listen, what is the mystery? I have, for more than a month, prowled, spun around, run about. And in my absence, alas, what has happened? My eyes are opening at last. Lucas is coming. I leave you. Until we meet again.

(Exit Girard.)

Widow

Go to whatever hurries you.

(Enter Lucas.)

Lucas

O fortune, fortune, when will I catch you? You always fly from me.

Widow

Always fortune on the brain?

Lucas

Yes, for it hates me. I do this, I do that—labor all my life. Labor for this one, labor for that one. I work for thirty years. After thirty years, here I am. To labor for another, it's small palliative. To work for oneself, that takes courage. To even everything up, wouldn't it be right for the others, in their turn, to work for me?

Widow

Lucas wishes to reach the heights.

Lucas

Suddenly, yes, to find myself there, as in a miracle. I've got the character for it—no matter how hazardous. I gamble, win some, lose some; it's only that it doesn't make one happy. I've played double or nothing out of boredom. I have forty tickets for this lottery.

Widow

That's a very prudent way to place money.

Lucas

Yeah. Because I love big lotteries. I am going to make my fortune that way.

Widow

You will make your fortune through your daughter. The Baron loves her more and more.

Lucas

He's becoming hot. But my daughter lacks the feeling to marry him.

Widow

She's shrewd and subtle.

Lucas

It's beginning to make him keen.

Widow

And, the Baron, who's only a village Baron, hasn't, as you know, much brains.

Lucas

Not necessary to say he's stupid, because all the world knows it well. But Lisette can hear us. Come on, daughter, come on. Madam and I were talking about how your wit satisfies her. She said you were so subtle, said you were so knowing.

(Enter Lisette, listening.)

Lisette (pretending naiveté)

Father, I don't know what she thinks of me.

Lucas

So much the worse, my daughter, so much the worse.

Widow

Today, you've joined some ornament to your simple country dress.

Lisette

It's to please the Baron, as you advised me. I am making myself over to be loved. I am obedient, and I intend, to please you, that he marry me quickly. So, that's why I added to my costume today.

Widow

You'd have made him love you, that's already done. But to make him marry you, you must double-dose him with sighs, looks, and little manners. Put to work my recent lessons. We shall try to please at first by simple attractions. A little affectation, lowering your gaze, being quiet, appearing embarrassed. A cold-blooded man, seeing a great deal of simpering, will believe less what he sees. He will suspect, examine, and discover the pretence. But, when the dupe is taken—be affected without fear. The grossest kinds of affection, far from quelling, charm his passions, and he seeks out the beauty of nature.

Lucas

I don't understand half your fine preaching. (dumbfounded) But what you say must be good, for you amaze.

Widow

Lisette understands perfectly.

Lisette

Not so much as you think. You have taught me well, speaking to me of these looks which make women so refined. But I am not so refined. I cannot do as they do.

Widow

Oh, you will go far. You know how to please, and how to pretend.

Lisette

You deceive yourself. I contradict myself in no respect. I please the Baron without feigning to please him. If he is deceived, I can never be. When I speak contrary to my thought, one can see in my manner that I am embarrassed.

Widow

The Baron could, by a tender turnabout, mention again the contract he made the other day. He is changeable, peevish in his tenderness, thinks to profit by his day of weakness. Has he promised again today?

Lisette

Alas, no.

Widow

He must have thought it over. It's his day to be reasonable, his good day. But we will recapture him. To make him sign, it's only needful to make him wait. If something can hasten this happy day, it's pretence. Pretend a violent love.

Lisette

Alas, I will pretend badly.

Widow

Then, I am uneasy. I intend to marry as much as Lisette. Monsieur Argon occupies me and I am going to see him. If he keeps his word, it will be all over today. (exits)

Lucas

You must pretend, the widder lady says, and you don't know how to pretend a pretense. You say everything that comes into your head and that's a mistake. Have the virtue to lie a bit. You don't know how, and that upsets me.

Lisette

Oh, console yourself, father. If I am still stupid, I am not really stupid. I know how to pretend better than the Widow thinks. I have some tricks she hasn't seen yet. If I always tell her I am innocent, and that, despite her lessons, I am ignorant, it's all on purpose so she will be proud of me.

Lucas

Oh, you know what you're doing and I cannot complain of you.

Lisette

You are going to see how I intend to make a fortune.

Lucas

Fortune is our master.

Lisette

It is true—it is our master. But, if he should fail me?

Lucas

Ha! Ha! I see well what you intend. So as not to lack one, you will have two.

Lisette

Yes, at least, father. That's what I'm doing. But the other has less wealth, which annoys me. For Monsieur Baron—here's what I fear—his conversation does not entirely please me. I have spoken to him a lot, pretending to be innocent. No, for marriage he has no plans. He says he wants to stay single for ten more years.

Lucas

To remain single—oh, oh. He wants to marry you so you can remain a virgin?

Lisette

To understand him, the loves of a nobleman for girls like me does us much honor.

Lucas

No, no, of these nobles, love without marriage takes honor from girls that nothing gives back.

Lisette

One has much wealth, but he will deceive me. The other hasn't very much, but he will marry me.

Lucas

The other is this Girard, correct?

Lisette

Fie!

Lucas

I'll say fie to him. If he comes round, I'll kick him out.

Lisette

Kick him out? Ah, be careful. Let him be in love—that costs nothing. If the others fail, he may make his fortune. Who knows?

Lucas

Well said. So, there's to be three for one. But, who is the new one who you say is certain?

Lisette

If he marries me, the Widow will be very chagrined.

Lucas (astonished by degrees
and then understanding)

The Devil!

Lisette

I will take her chance.

Lucas

Death!

Lisette

For I will break her marriage.

Lucas

Astounding!

Lisette

It is going to astonish you. For I will have the wealth intended for her. I will marry her lover.

Lucas (crying out)

My Lord! You will ruin her. She loves you as if you were her daughter.

Lisette

Can I do otherwise? I said no at first. I really would have preferred not to wrong her. But she has given me lessons in fortune hunting. I've got to take advantage of my youth like others. The other lesson she gave me recently was to love at first for one's profit. I love the Widow, but—

Lucas

But, you are able to love what profits you? These lessons are her own fault, and she deserves it.

Lisette

I'm in despair. At bottom, I have a good heart. I would prefer for her to marry the Baron.

Lucas

Yes, for he's more rich and you will gain by the change. In the case of the three lovers, here's how it goes: the Baron's worth more than Argon, he's got six times his money. Argon's better, worth more than Girard, and Girard's better than nothing.

Lisette

He's like nothing, yes, but with respect to the other two, we will keep your plans and mine secret.

Lucas

Yes, better to be secret. For these two good spouses won't be married, if they know about each other.

Lisette

The Baron's returning.

Lucas

Yes, I am going to do what you told me.

Lisette

Pretend to be enraged. We must see if he will marry me.

(Enter Baron.)

Lucas

Oh, that's definitive. He'll marry you to death, for he looks thoughtful.

Baron

Lucas intends to leave me. This disturbs me. How can I bear not to see Lisette any more?

Lisette (after having spoken low)

Yell very loud, then leave without speaking to him.

Lucas (loud so that the Baron hears)

Yes, I intend to leave our master, and I'm going to start going about it.

Lisette (pretending to be very angry to leave the Baron)

No! Don't leave him!

Lucas

I have told him, and I am no traitor. I told him of it a while ago, and I'm going.

Lisette

To leave to find a master!

Lucas

As you are growing up, it's a cruelty to stay here. In a village, you lose your time and your beauty. You can merchandise your youth better in the Paris marriage market. Yes, I will take you to Paris, and very soon, because time presses. Although a vertigo irritates me momentarily. What I want is only reasonable, and I shall be as bold as brass. (pushing his hat onto his head and passing before the Baron) I am upset to leave him, but 'death, I shall console myself. (exits)

Baron

He was very abrupt with me on a frivolous subject. Has he gone crazy? What can he intend to do?

Lisette (twisting her handkerchief)

I will never see you anymore. I am in despair.

Baron

There's always some shadow maiming fortune.

Lisette

He's wrong, for, sir, I see what he is hoping.

Baron

He would suddenly become a great lord.

Lisette (looking tenderly at the Baron)

Yes, to see me a great lady, and that is my misfortune. He imagines something that can't be. The daughter of a farmer is not for his master.

Baron

You will be with me as if you were my own child.

Lisette

Oh, sir, that's not what he has in mind.

Baron

I believe he intends to pay me less rent.

Lisette

He intends something far different.

Baron

Yes, what a repayment.

Lisette (starting to cry)

No, that's not what one day you said, that day you were full of love for me. You intended, you said, to write a promise. You no longer love me!

Baron

That day was like today. My feelings were full for you. I love you, Lisette.

Lisette

And, if I still must leave?

Baron

Of my love, you will have a sure pledge. A contract.

Lisette (stopping her tears)

Today?

Baron

A marriage contract. It's already written. I did it right away, first thing. Second thing is to sign.

Lisette

You won't sign it?

Baron

I will sign.

Lisette

But, when? For my father is taking me off. He is so proud.

Baron

My word is reliable.

Lisette

I believe you, but my father—

Baron

Yes, I will give you my oath.

Lisette (crying again)

Don't swear to me. I believe you already. But my father—

Baron

I will go appease him. I swear to you.

Lisette (crying and holding him by the arm)

No, he's going to take me off. Of that I am sure.

Baron

No, no. I am going to keep Lucas.

Lisette (pretending to be outré with rage against him)

It's I who wish to leave, because you don't love me!

(Exit Baron.)

Lisette (suddenly stops crying)

No—this is only a deceiver, who thinks me innocent. I must soon take my relative, the Widow's, lover. He has no wealth. That's my last resource. But, he's coming to the garden to speak to me. Let's continue. I played the naïve and tender. Now to play the dreamer.

(Enter Argon.)

Argon

Yes, Lisette is going to return. (he turns to look closely at her) How pretty she is, dreaming. How many charms I see. She sighs. Good! I feel that she is for me. What are you dreaming of?

(Lisette, after having let Argon look her over, pretends to be astonished to see Argon so near her.)

Lisette

Oh! You've startled me so! I was dreaming—that I have so much freedom—suddenly in the garden.

Argon

That's what charmed me. You've already told me, not that I am loved, but that you will soon love me.

Lisette

I am confused by what you are thinking. I ask pardon. To love you would be to lack respect for you.

Argon

Lack respect? Yes, I intend to. A too respectful love obtains nothing.

Lisette

But, I don't love. Speak more. Encourage me, then.

Argon

To give you courage, I make a contract; but, complete my wishes.

(The Widow enters and listens.)

Argon

Add a word to your looks, your sighs. This word is a great word. Tell me—"I love you."

Lisette

I've told you a hundred times—and to myself, a thousand.

Argon

To yourself?

Lisette

Alas, yes.

Argon

What naiveté!

Lisette

Why hide it from you if it is the truth?

Argon

Behold love. Behold pure sincerity. This calls me to love, like nature. There, Lisette, here's the role I have taken. I intend to take you, in secret, to Paris, for I will, at first, marry you secretly. Let's hide all from the Widow. She would be jealous of it. I will marry you without her knowing anything of it. In her place, in a word, you will have all my wealth.

Lisette

I want nothing from you but your person. Give her all your wealth.

Argon

But, if I give it to her, what will the two of us and our children live on?

Lisette

I don't want it for myself, but you'll need it.

Argon (taking her hand)

There, let us separate. No, stay here.

Lisette

I am staying.

Argon

Go—and be in the nearby woods in an hour. (he kisses her hand) Go quickly. Wait! The marriage is made.

Lisette (perceiving the Widow)

Ah! All is discovered.

Argon

I am an indiscreet fool!

(Exit Lisette.)

Widow

What have I heard? I am struck mute with shock!

Argon

And I! I am mute with shame. From frankness, I am going to admit to you that what you have seen—I am wrong. The marriage I contracted with you ought to prevent me from making another. But, as friendship alone made ours, it would seem love is stronger. Still, I was wrong to betray you thus. But, if you know how Lisette loves me, from friendship for me, you yourself would say—marry her, sir, I freely consent. What pleasure, at my age of fifty-four years, to be loved for myself. Yes, only for my person. For she refused my wealth which I would give, only wanting me. But, I am doubly wrong to betray you, to anger you. From prudence, I ought never to speak of Lisette. Yes, Madam, I am wrong, a hundred times wrong. But she will be my wife.

Widow

I cannot recover. This blow is overwhelming. I excuse Argon. At bottom, he loves blindly. As for me, I really deserve for Lisette to deceive me. But, for this marriage—it is necessary that I break it. Were the good Argon never to marry me— Let us try to disabuse him—from friendship.

CURTAIN

ACT II

The Widow is overwhelmed with chagrin. Girard is holding in his hand a packet of letters for the Baron. He separates one letter and substitutes another.

Girard

Without breaking the seal, and without compromising myself, I half-open the Baron's letter and replace the false with the true. My hand trembles, for this is my first attempt in falseness.

Widow (dreaming, not listening)

Argon will marry Lisette?

Girard

He will never marry my charming coquette. This will see to him—as I told you.

Widow

Very good! But, let me digest my spite. The one who married me, marries my coquette. Was this what I raised Lisette for? With impunity, Lisette has played me this trick, when I instructed her to pretend love. I was the plaything of her apprenticeship. I thought she would absorb no malice from the instruction I gave her. Just a little grain of it for perfection. I ought to have realized from my own example, that malice, once seeded in a woman's heart, profits, multiplies, and grows like weeds.

Girard

In malice, Lisette is fertile, yet I love her, I adore her, and I will make her my wife. But, what am I saying? I ought to remember, Madam—(ironically) that you don't give Lisette to Girard. As I am only a tax collector, I ought through respect for you, her, and myself, to let her marry your lover.

Widow

At her age, to manage, under my eyes, three lovers at the same time! Coquettes of Paris and coquettes of the country—some ready language, some trickery. My word, all is equal for coquetry.

Girard (ironically)

You intended to give her to some great lord.

Widow

Ah, I will give her to the devil, with all my heart.

Girard

I beg you for preference over him at least.

Widow

So be it, but at least provide me some confidence that you will succeed.

Girard

You know all. We must lure our credulous, stupid, avaricious, and amorous Baron with this false lottery into offering Lisette marriage, and if she accepts, for Argon to see she's engaged.

Widow

Lisette ought to give up Argon for the Baron. The Baron is rich and the trick is so good.

Girard

Yes, but I mustn't lose Lisette.

Widow

If Argon is undeceived, I will be satisfied.

Girard

May he see her half-married to the Baron.

Widow

Completely married, if necessary.

Girard

Completely? Hell, no!

Widow

He's coming.

Girard

My insurance, which I well know how to use—

(Enter Baron. Girard presents a packet to the Baron.)

Girard

I am returning from the post office and I have the honor to give the gentleman what he asked me to bring.

(Exit Girard.)

Baron (to Widow)

Neighbor, my love is going to make me despair. Lisette intends to leave.

Widow

I take the place of mother to her. I guarantee her tender, wise, and sincere. You don't know how much she is worth. She wants a contract, that's her only fault. And, you don't wish to make one.

Baron

I intend to marry her. Who told you otherwise? But, to do such a thing, the later the better. I will marry when I am much older.

Widow

Eh! You are old enough, sir, for a wife.

Baron

I am very irresolute. I blame myself for it. Ha, ha, good, this letter is from one of my friends. It's for the lottery we've all subscribed to.

Widow

Is it, then, published?

Baron

Yes, exactly. It's the list.

Widow

I am sure to win. A physiognomist has seen great sums of money on my face. What I must do, he told me, to earn it, is to buy a lottery. It's the most prompt way to win for a wise woman.

Baron

Hum! Hum! I know, by heart, the puzzle of each. The numbers, the names, I don't see one. Let's read—ah!

Widow

What's the matter?

Baron

Something I see irritates me.

Widow

What is it, then? From where does this sudden dolor come?

Baron

Lucas: one hundred thousand francs.

Widow

To the farmer, the Grand Prize? But, let's see. Reread it. Is it, indeed, his name? Lucas?

Baron

I am not the master of my scorn.

Widow

Grand Prize to Lucas? You are ruining us, traitor.

Baron

To Lucas, the Grand Prize.

Widow

You won't allow it. Oh, Fate, unjust Fate, that Lucas be enriched.

Baron

I cannot recover. His good fortune desolates me.

Widow (pretending a quick thought, accompanied by joy)

But, let us rejoice and laugh.

Baron

Are you crazy?

Widow

No, at first we both had a stupid inspiration. It's surprised us.

Baron

Well?

Widow

You are angry that chance has just enriched Lisette's fortune. Fortune, on the contrary, is favoring you. It has determined to make you happy.

Baron

Oh, oh!

Widow

For the money, and without any love, these days, the most noble marry Lisettes.

Baron

Right, one hundred thousand francs would pay off my debts. This motive and love will excuse all.

Widow

Yes, but you must marry instantly, before this lottery becomes known. This is delicacy. She will believe she owes your all the more tenderness. Lucas will get the Grand Prize, but while he is unaware of it, the fool must be taken, so that he gives all his wealth to Lisette. Wealth, present and to come.

Baron

Yes, but be discreet. I will say that I am taking Lisette without a sou.

Widow

The joke is that everybody will believe you're a fool.

(Enter Lisette.)

Baron

Here, Lisette, here.

(The Widow goes to find Lisette, who listens from the depths of the theatre.)

Widow

Your fortune is made, Lisette. It is I who am procuring it. Hug me, Lisette.

Baron

Your tears have softened me, Lisette. I surrender. Let's sign the contract as quickly as I can inform the notary.

Lisette (aside, while the Widow and the Baron talk in low voices)

Do they wish to deceive me? For I understand nothing. (she dreams profoundly)

(Enter Argon.)

Argon (aside)

An explanation would be very nice here.

Lisette

Ah, here they both are. All is lost. What to do?

Argon (to the Baron)

What did Girard warn me? But, it's your custom. I've often seen you boast of love. You believe yourself loved by Lisette, then, sir?

Baron

The proof of this is that I am making her my wife.

Argon

Girard made no mistake. You intend to overwhelm her with your wealth. But she cannot betray her love for me.

Baron

She hasn't any love for you. I swear it.

Argon

It's you who flatter yourself to a fault, I assure you.

Baron

I tell you, she has never loved anyone but me.

Argon

I am sure of her heart and her good faith. Decide between us to finish the dispute.

Baron

I disdain it. Repeat for the one hundredth time that you love me tenderly.

Lisette

Me, tell you that? Truly, I take little care, sir. It is from respect that I let you speak. I believed, at first, that you were boasting, to laugh. But, without offending you, sir, I will tell you, I have no love for you, nor will I ever have.

Baron

What? Why?

Widow

What does she say? Ah, how great is my shock!

Baron

What do you say?

Argon

Must she tell you again?

Baron

What? Haven't you said a hundred times that you love me?

Lisette

Me? No.

Argon (charmed)

What naiveté.

Widow (angry that Lisette has not fallen into the trap)

What do I hear?

Baron

What? Your tears, your sighs?

Lisette

Were lies.

Argon

I know my neighbor. Without a doubt, it is a dream that he has seen you in tears and heaving sighs. At his age, while sleeping, these are pleasant notions.

Baron

But, I haven't dreamed what you have written.

Lisette

It's my father, and Madam is there to tell you so.

Widow

I am enraged.

Argon

I know Lucas is ambitious. He prefers your wealth, for you're worth more to him. But, besides, I believe her—what likelihood is there that Lisette, who always says what she thinks, has spoken to you of love, when she loves me?

Lisette

What are you saying, sir? I have believed, in good faith, that you spoke in jest that you love me; but this joke is not true.

Argon

Eh—what?

Widow (aside, delighted)

What is her plan? Does she dream, or is it I who dream?

Argon

It's in vain that you still think the secret is necessary. (to Baron) We made a secret of our love. (to Lisette) Speak, I permit you to speak freely.

Lisette

If you permit me to speak freely, I don't love you.

Widow

She's frank enough about that.

Argon

How indignant I am!

Baron

By God, I've my revenge.

Argon

But, I understand nothing. Speak clearly, I wish it. Tell them that you intended to manage us both.

Lisette

I had no intention of managing either of you, I assure you, and you can see it quite well.

Widow

That's speaking plainly.

Lisette

For, hold on, I prefer my liberty, a hundred times, to all your grand honors and quality. To be the wife of a great lord, I would be a servant. As for your kindnesses, of which I am cognizant, pardon me if I refuse them. In a word, both of you wish to marry me, but I will never marry either one of you.

Baron

There's your dismissal.

Argon

It is also yours.

Baron

I cannot recover from my astonishment.

Argon

Leave her, forget her, that's sufficient to punish her.

Baron

Well said. No more love.

Argon

Yes, we scorn Lisette.

Baron (to Widow)

She has a hundred thousand francs which I still regret.

Widow (low)

Keep it up your sleeve. We are going to speak to her.

Argon (low)

Madam.

Widow

Well, sir?

Argon

Would you go get a notary to come to your house? We are going to conclude our business instantly.

(Argon exits.)

Widow (to Baron, low)

He abandons her, for you that's the main thing. I am going to rid you of a rival.

Baron

No, I don't understand at all.

Widow

Neither do I. But, prudence dictates that one go in the greatest hurry.

(Exit Baron and Widow. Argon returns from the other side, and looks to see if the Widow sees him.)

Lisette (dreaming, alone)

I think—yes, from what I've seen, I've done well, I believe. When they are with me, by themselves, as they will be, I will know what to do to have them back.

Argon (aside)

The Widow is already far away. Let's penetrate this mystery. From scorn, I have banished all animosity. I return solely from curiosity, to see what reasons you will have to give me.

Lisette

Permit me to laugh, seeing you so angry. What? Didn't you see what my plan was?

Argon (enraged)

No, I didn't see it, and all subterfuge is in vain.

Lisette

I told the Baron the truth, without ruse or subterfuge, for fear he would continue in his mistake. I didn't wish to deceive him.

Argon (still enraged)

I understand perfectly. But, why speak to me as to him? To refuse me? Me? Me?

Lisette

Let's talk about him first. You see me delighted. I have punished that liar the way I have quite wanted to.

Argon (still enraged)

But me, me?

Lisette

Patience. He wanted to marry me today, and my father is on his side. And you wanted the jealous Widow to see that I love you and will marry you. If they knew that I can love you, they would get me locked up.

Argon

Ha! Ha!

Lisette

Truly, I would have completely spoiled the mystery. You told me yourself before to keep quiet.

Argon

You've done very properly. Yes, you're right, and I am the fool. To deceive the Baron—yes, I see the pretense is prudent and useful.

Lisette

I believe, too, well done, at least.

Argon

How charming Lisette is. I am not blind, I see clearly that Lisette prefers me to a far richer man. What love! What wit!

Lisette

I have no wit. Love has added to my customary want of it.

Argon

We must secretly—

Lisette

Yes, but let's separate. I will go alone, in secret, to your place for a short while.

Argon

Without your father—

Lisette

He's coming. Leave me, for I tremble if the Baron and he should see us together.

(Exit Argon. Enter Lucas and the Baron.)

Lisette (aside)

Here I am sure of one, but he's my second choice. Let's retake the other one. He's back to speak to me.

Lucas

She must have gone crazy, and what she said astonishes me. You say she doesn't love you and refuses to be a Baroness?

Baron (to Lisette)

You have just revived my wrath. Ah, how I ought to kill my love for you. How can you, at your age, have the audacity to give me the lie—me, and look in my face, and tell me that you don't love me?

Lisette (pretending to have a grudge against him)

Yes, I have maintained it to your face, for it is true.

Baron

Without doubt, it happened unexpectedly to you, some vapor which disturbed your senses and memory. For how else could I believe that, after the ardent love you've shown me?

Lisette (adding to her simulated scorn)

I never loved you.

Baron

Still? I am outraged. You have told me a hundred times, and before your father.

Lisette

I never said it to you.

Baron

She makes me despair.

Lisette (softening)

No, never, or at least—

Baron

At least?

Lisette

If I said it, I repent it so much. I have so much scorn, that if I said it, I will say the contrary, always to the whole wide world, to yourself, to my father. (pretending tenderness) What the world will know, that I loved you, and that, when I cried from love, you didn't want to marry me. No, no, and against you, my courage has returned. Me! I love you? I would indeed have little heart. My love was honest and yours was deceitful.

Lucas (who has softened, taken in and almost crying)

I've seen—she's right.

Baron

Then it's from rage, suspecting my love is not sincere, that you have told me you don't love me?

Lisette

Yes, exactly. Am I wrong?

Baron

You love me then?

Lisette

Alas!

Baron

Let's forget all this, Lisette, let's go quickly to a notary. May a contract be the prize of your sincere love. Let's hurry.

(Exit Baron.)

Lucas (transported with joy)

Quickly, quickly!

Lisette (low to her father, holding him by the arm)

Let's go softly.

Lucas

I'm going to be papa to a Baroness.

Lisette

Oh, I doubt it.

Lucas

Why? He's making you his wife and says so.

Lisette

No, I can see some trick.

Lucas

He marries, and that's that.

Lisette

I don't believe a word of it, father.

Lucas

To not believe the wedding, when it's come?

Lisette

I believe he's deceiving me. First, I saw the Widow when Argon spoke of the business in a fret with Girard. Raging, despairing—and now she's just embraced me; knowing that I deceived her, she comes to caress me.

Lucas

Yes, it's treason.

Lisette

The Baron refused me. Then, suddenly, he changes and wants me.

Lucas

It's a trick.

Lisette (after having dreamed)

If the Widow and Girard, who know how to trick, said to the Baron: pretend to marry her and as soon as she agrees, won't Argon be disgusted?

Lucas

Oh—that's it! I see clearly.

Lisette (dreaming again)

For me, I don't see. For, on the other side, perhaps the Baron really wanted to marry me. That would embarrass, no, yes, the more I think about it— May I have enough wit and not be too clever by half.

Lucas

Listen to my good advice. I have marvelous ideas. For, in the state where things are perilous, you have wit, but in a family affair, a father, as they say, is older than his daughter. Here then is my good advice. Let's go find the Baron. He's the most important.

Lisette

No.

Lucas

No?

Lisette

No.

Lucas

It's the second who is good. Let's go find Argon.

Lisette

No.

Lucas

Then I don't know any more than an animal? Oh, my third advice, it's to have a tête-à-tête.

Lisette

Go find the Baron alone.

Lucas

Yes, I understand.

Lisette

And, I alone am going to find Mr. Argon. You finish one side, I will finish the other.

Lucas

Wow! That's very good. I will marry them both before the notary.

Lisette

As for me, when both contracts are drawn up—I will see. The first one to sign—that's the one I'll take.

Lucas

You will take hastily. It's the chance of the game. Let's sign two contracts soon, for fear we will lack one.

Lisette

Mr. Argon's waiting for me. I'm off.

(Exit Lisette.)

Lucas (alone)

Go, quick, go. But how can she get that all out of her own head? I believe she must have two brains, for she always amazes me. Yes, she's only my daughter. By God, her wit is already far ahead of mine.

(Enter Girard)

Girard (aside)

Let's latch on to the father. I risk nothing, for without him the Baron can conclude nothing. By making him read this phony list, let us disturb his head. Let's throw the dice. (counterfeiting the newsboys) Lists, lists of winners!

Lucas

Lottery winners! Let's see a bit. What did you say there?

Girard

Let's see if this lottery came out good.

Lucas

What do I see there? Don't I see the seal?

Girard

Clever. Are you curious? (putting the list on the side where Lucas is not) Read here.

Lucas

Very well. But show me better then.

Girard

To an avaricious reader—oh beautiful thought. May a happy fool with a lucky number—

Lucas

Ha, ha, that's it!

Girard

Yes, it is. Hum, hum.

Lucas

Let's see that.

Girard (turning the list to the other side)

With pleasure. Let's see.

Lucas

Eh! I can't see anything that way.

Girard (turning the other side even worse)

Let's read. Let's see. Ah!

(Girard is moving and raising and lowering the paper so Lucas can't see.)

Lucas (with a little joy)

What is it? Show me then, friend.

Girard

No. I was mistaken. But, hum, hum. I hope—(letting Lucas see the paper) God, I don't see a thing.

Lucas

Ah, by God, I see. Let's see quickly there, Girard. I see something about me.

Girard (hiding the list)

No, it's nothing at all.

Lucas (joyfully)

And I have seen. My name is there!

Girard

Take it easy. You probably have won nothing. I will give you a hundred francs at best.

Lucas

No, no. I've seen what I've seen. Lucas, it's my name.

Girard

If you have, at least I want to be reimbursed. Return my money, it's my only resource.

Lucas

All right. Show quickly.

Girard

It's one of the numbers. It's at least a thousand francs. I have seen several zeroes.

Lucas

Several zeroes? I intend to see as many as grains of sand.

Girard

You're a man insatiable for zeroes.

Lucas (joyous)

Ah, it's ten thousand francs.

Girard

Curious, yes, I see. But, if that isn't the numeral?

Lucas

By God, I'm really frightened.

Girard

Let's confirm.

Lucas (thoughtful)

Yes, there it is, the fifth.

Girard (giving the list)

Read it over, and calculate it yourself.

Lucas (taking the list, upset)

My heart beats—beats. I am quite transported. I'm afraid to have seen double, and to have counted too many. One, two, three, four, and five.

Girard

Let's say—

Lucas (upset)

One, two, three, did I say three?

Girard

Yes.

Lucas

Ah, I see the number that's formed. I'm a bit overwhelmed.

Girard

In short, Lucas has the Grand Prize?

Lucas

Ouf!

Girard (relaxing)

Relax. Take off your coat.

Lucas

The Grand Prize!

Girard

Since one is rich, one must get a little better clothes.

Lucas

One hundred thousand francs!

Girard

How much we'll drink at Lucas' place!

Lucas

Let's go quickly to Paris.

Girard

I will get you a carriage and horses.

Lucas

Ah, I believe I'll die of luxury. Let's see the lottery quickly, so I can see myself first again.

Girard

Are you going to remain a farmer?

Lucas (indignant)

Me! A farmer.

Girard

Forgive me for saying the word. I quite see the question is crazy. Well, give me your rents. You won't want them. You'll be a great lord. I am a poor devil, and your loyal friend. You will give them to me for this good news.

Lucas

Yes. Get me a carriage and horses that go very fast, very fast.

Girard

Yes, like birds. But, at first, in passing, let's stop at the notary to give me the rents. All right, father?

Lucas

Yes, I won't need it myself. I will leave you all the rents from my timberland. I am going straight to Paris to get some nobility.

CURTAIN

ACT III

Argon is trying to avoid showing himself to the Widow, who grabs him by the arm.

Widow

I will prove it all to you. Can you doubt it? But, stay one minute, at least to listen to me.

Argon

Time presses. I have Lisette and the notary together. If Lucas appears, I will finish the business. In love, moments are precious to an older person.

Widow

If you marry, a quarter of an hour later, you will have time to be tired of Lisette and to repent a foolish act. Pardon the word, it's from friendship for you. My zeal is not mixed with any jealous transport. Better if you never marry me or the coquette. Be undeceived and I will be satisfied. Eh—can you remain blind? I will prove to both you and the Baron how she trapped you, at once reconciling, by the same management, traitorous simplicity and naïve lies. By the cleverest tricks and the most lively manners, she's figured out how to get love without giving any. She coldbloodedly talks in the most tender way and pretends with effrontery to be timidly embarrassed. Tears which go right to the heart and which bother her not at all. She abuses his weakness and yours. In offering you one hand, she gives him the other. Thus, a coquette delivers perfidy with both hands, and if she needs it, will find another hand for a third.

Argon

You've said it twenty times. But for the hundredth time, you still must prove it.

Widow

Speak low. I see the Baron and Lucas. Keep aside and you will perhaps be able to see that not only Lucas prefers his master to you, but also Lisette.

Argon

Let's see. I would be undeceived.

(Argon goes to the side. Enter Girard.)

Widow

Well?

Girard

Lucas is occupied with his Grand Prize.

Widow

But, does the Baron intend to marry—

Girard

Patience. I am given all the rents in advance. For it is I who have managed all. Lucas is metamorphosed into a great lord. Since he has seen the lottery, his sudden riches trouble his head, and have changed his type. He has nothing human remaining except his form and his pride. Grave, deciding with a wink of his eye, disdaining to speak, or speaking by sentence. He believes people applaud his silence. Saluting with his big head, puffed up, swollen, Lucas has become subtly inflated with a contagious disease. He can be seen thrusting his paunch two steps ahead of himself.

Widow

In that case, Girard, we must— But Lisette is running this way. Mr. Argon is following her. Things aren't turning out right.

Girard

No.

Widow

I am going to join Argon right away. Amuse these two here.

Girard

All that one plans, does not succeed.

(Exit Widow. Lucas is walking in grandly. The Baron, hat in hand, follows Lucas, who puts his hat back on first.)

Baron

Yes, I beam with pleasure that fortune has fulfilled your wish.

Lucas

Although my fortune may be much higher than yours, I would be father and companion to you, always. (slaps him on the shoulder) For I am not proud.

Baron

Indeed, I see that, Lucas.

Girard

You see that the gentleman doesn't underrate himself. He deserves to fill a great office.

Lucas

Haven't you retained a fine place for me at the Post? For that's why I am going to Paris.

Girard

I already told you, they're looking for a carriage softer than a bed for you.

Lucas

But, what's keeping the carriage? I don't want to have to wait.

Girard

The horses will soon be here at your orders. Wait for them here. Hola, lackey, hola, some chairs.

(Lackeys enter with chairs. Lucas exchanges greetings with the Baron and seats himself first.)

Lucas

Let's not have any manners while I'm here.

Baron

Let's talk about our business.

Lucas (not replying)

I've got a great idea just now.

Baron

We were discussing—

Lucas

In seeing me, all Paris is going to feast me. The one who won the Grand Prize.

Baron

Before you leave—

Lucas

All the world will be beggars except me, because my wealth will divert me. While I am in the grain, I am going to see people cry famine. What a pleasure!

Baron

Then, Lucas, do you intend to reach a conclusion for my ardent love?

Lucas

They're going to propose to me some pretty expenses, pretty horses, and pretty families to marry into. This business will increase wealth. I'll buy whatever's for sale.

Girard

But, to ennoble you, you would have a gentleman for a son-in-law.

Baron

Lisette is waiting for us.

Lucas

I'll have all this, indeed, for when one is very rich, one attracts all that for nothing.

Baron

You promised me—

Lucas (with an important air)

Huh!

Baron

To finish—

Lucas

What?

Baron

Our business.

Lucas

What business?

Baron

Ours, I have had the notary there, to write the contract. He's waiting only for you. We are agreed between us.

Lucas

Ah, I believe that I remember something of it. Damn, when one has so much business, one thinks only of the best. Yes, we spoke of marriage, but it cannot be. There's only, but a bit—

Girard

What do I hear? What, then, you already intend to disown it?

Baron

Remember, Lucas, that I was your master.

Girard

Lucas, remember that there's great honor, a handsome alliance to have a lord for a son-in-law.

Lucas

Oh, it's money which makes the best marriages.

Baron

What, you no longer intend?

Lucas

I want no part of your lineage.

Baron

What?

Lucas

But, it's necessary to listen to me. I am a native of this hamlet. That means, that from friendship, I love your earth, your château. Yet, it's not mine if you become my son-in-law. My opinion is it would be better if you sold it to me.

Baron

You're joking, I believe. Sell you my château?

Lucas

It is all dilapidated, but I will make a lot of improvements.

Baron

He's gone crazy.

Girard (low)

This rascal scorns you.

Lucas

The land will ennoble me. That's what I want of you. While at Paris I increase my money, you keep the land fallow.

Girard

You will be his farmer.

Baron (rising)

This is too much insolence.

Girard (to Baron)

Sir, calm down. I promise you revenge.

Lucas (aside, also rising)

This little gentleman, he heard all that. He owes money everywhere, but he believes he is to be respected. But, I will have his château. He'd better leave. He has some creditors. I will have it through the law.

Girard (after having spoken low to the Baron)

We have done all, sir, for your good. But to revenge yourself, better say nothing.

(Enter Lisette.)

Lisette

I have been looking for you everywhere. Ouf! I'm out of breath. To find you, father, took a lot of trouble. I have run—for they say—but I don't believe it—I heard it everywhere—the Grand Prize. These are the compliments that greet me everywhere. They say a hundred thousand francs. Is it true, father?

Lucas

True.

Lisette (impressed)

A hundred thousand francs!

(Enter Argon and the Widow.)

Argon (who runs after her)

Well, are you fleeing from me? Speak! Since you've heard about the lottery, and you know the news, you scorn me.

Lisette

Yes.

Argon

This is a handsome fortune. But, it ought not to attract your scorn to me. Answer me, at least. Will you marry me?

Lisette

I obey my father. He has told me that he wishes to defer this business. (low to Lucas and making a sign with her eyes to him) Tell him that it's you who refuse.

Lucas

Good, good.

Lisette

That costs nothing. Get me off.

Lucas

No.

Lisette (signaling with her eyes)

Tell them something that will end my engagement, at least.

Lucas

Eh! You trouble yourself too much about them. Leave off your winking. Not necessary for any polish. You have what you need to marry.

Widow

Her father covets her, the opulent fool. Foolishness that he doesn't try to excuse.

Argon

By her own fault, she herself disabused me. As for me, so as not to risk another love trick, I'm engaging myself to you.

Widow

Friendship without love. That's what we agree makes a good marriage. Love is restless and bores itself in a household.

Baron

You would have had our wealth. You will be confounded.

Lucas

Let them say—then you will have three times more, four times more.

Lisette

Let's go quickly to Paris to be in abundance.

Lucas

Between the land and our money—there's the difference. Their land and their château. It's nothing but a little plot. It will never increase, no, not even an abortion. But my money is in a great adventure. It will swell at first, and then like a river, it will increase.

Lisette

Increase.

Lucas

Increase—it will increase.

Lisette

Ah, how I will have lovers who will respect me. What happiness! I will see brilliant fortunes. What a following I am going to have. Lackeys, servants.

Girard

And valets de chambre—for page—Girard.

Lucas

Let them bring on my horses.

Widow

They will harness you a carriage.

Girard

Go on foot, from fear that your carriage will break down. This is going to reform the pomp of your train. (giving the list to Lisette) This is the true list.

Widow

Yes, the reversal is very afflicting. But you've shone already for your money. A hundred thousand francs for you in the air.

Baron

One hundred thousand francs to laugh at.

Lisette

What are they talking about? What?

Lucas (looking for the place where the prize was shown in his other list)

Eh! Go on, go on, let them talk. Here, here. It's here. For Lucas, the Grand Prize.

Baron

You will not buy my château, master fool.

Lucas (troubled)

It was there.

Girard

The zeroes are left.

Lisette

Oh! Father, they are mocking you.

Argon

Yes, here's the mystery.

Widow

You have nothing.

Girard

But nothing—gets nothing. I made the false list, and I found wealth. I've gotten all of Lucas' rents. My love for you makes heroic sacrifices. I give them all to you, Lisette.

Argon

Let's go to supper at my place.

Baron

Yes, let's go.

Girard

Yes, I have pity for the trouble in which I see you. These gentlemen, without their ranks. My offer ought to please you. They have made their fortune, and I have my fortune to make. But, I am, in a day, by myself, more amorous than the two of them can be in a month. They have not been able to acquire a young girl. But nobility acquires more than riches.

Lisette (to widow)

How much I owe you, Madam! It's you who turned my spirit upside down, in telling me that one must be a coquette.

Widow

I am well punished for my bad advice. I agree, I was wrong.

Lisette (to Girard)

I listened to her. You must have a Baron, she always said. No, I would never have thought of anyone but you, except for her. If I had followed my natural inclination, from tenderness I would have chosen you.

Girard

Eh! Choose me then! Lucas will consent.

Lucas (in going)

Ouf!

Girard

Speak!

Lucas

Ouf!

Girard

Two times ouf, in mute language, is worth one yes.

Widow

That's the fate of a coquette. After high prospects, one sees her, sooner or later, confused, confounded, and reduced to a Girard.

CURTAIN

THE CRAZY WAGER
WITH FLORENT DANCOURT

CAST OF CHARACTERS

Mrs. Hardwick

Phillip Hardwick

Angelica

Betty

Mr. Goodspeed, attorney

Tiffany, Hardwick's lackey

Tiggs

Jackson

Merlin

THE PLAY

MERLIN:

Well, Mr. Tiggs, how the devil did you get here? You've no business here.

TIGGS:

You don't know the half of it.

MERLIN:

Go in, and wait for me where I told you to.

TIGGS:

But the carriage?

MERLIN:

It's ready.

TIGGS:

Can't I wait here?

MERLIN:

No.

TIGGS:

My bonnet and my hairpiece?

MERLIN:

All your stuff is inside—go in, jackass, and leave me here.

TIGGS:

If anything is missing, the master will give me trouble.

MERLIN:

Nothing is missing, I tell you.

TIGGS:

In that case, goodbye.

MERLIN:

You must take Jackson with you.

TIGGS:

I will take him.

MERLIN:

Listen, listen up, I warned you to leave the mustaches alone.

TIGGS:

You did well to remind me. I had forgotten. Here, sir, I will wait on you with a firm step.

(Exit Tiggs, Enter Phillip Hardwick)

PHILLIP:

Oh, when will I see the end of all this? Will Angelica stay here longer, disguised as a man? I am impatient.

MERLIN:

Come, control yourself. The most violent hurry never advanced an affair one step.

PHILLIP:

With what coldness, with what prejudice my mother has refused to consent to my marriage—without wanting to know even the name of the family of the person I love.

MERLIN:

But, on the other hand, with what firmness, with what grandeur of soul, are you prepared to cheat her?

PHILLIP:

What reason could she have had?

MERLIN:

Sir, she wants to be young, despite her age, and letting you marry would make her a grandmother, and the name of a grandmother ages even a girl of fifteen.

PHILLIP:

It would indeed—yet.

MERLIN:

Oh, assuredly, it would have been better if she had understood, but on my soul, you are not of the body or humor to die without heirs—

PHILLIP:

My poor, Merlin, I intend to attempt the execution of our plan today.

MERLIN:

Then we must know the state of your mother's heart toward the supposed Count.

PHILLIP:

She loves him to fury, I tell you. Angelica is charming in this disguise.

MERLIN:

She's pleased with herself, and I don't know if she's in the same hurry you are to bring things to a conclusion.

PHILLIP:

As for me, I cannot live with this uncertainty.

MERLIN:

You'd do it sooner if you can convince your mother not to suspect my relationship to you.

PHILLIP:

Suspect it? We never see each other at my mother's house, and only meet when we are sure she cannot find us together.

MERLIN:

Frankly, she's a strange mother, and the strong aversion she has for you deserves the little trick we are about to play on her.

PHILLIP:

But do you believe that Tiggs has the wit?

MERLIN:

The wit? He's one of my pupils. He will play the false Marquise to a wonder, don't worry. Betty is in our interests, too.

PHILLIP:

I have done everything to expect it.

MERLIN:

Rest assured. And your mother's attorney?

PHILLIP:

I've conquered his scruples. He really cares about money.

MERLIN:

He's a fine fellow.

PHILLIP:

The best in the world. But he asked a hundred pounds for so good an office.

MERLIN:

A hundred pounds?—that's giving something for nothing. I'll extract the money from your mother and a bit more besides. If I had foreseen we'd need so much money, I'd have taken measures and the machine would be all set up.— Here's Betty.

PHILLIP:

(To Betty who enters) I was awaiting you with impatience. Well, my dear Betty, can you give me a full account of my mother's feelings? Has she opened her heart to you? Do you believe her passion strong enough?

BETTY:

It's beyond imagining, and I don't know if you ought not to repent having assisted in putting her in the state she is in.

PHILLIP:

What! Repent over a mother who, because she is mistress of all the family wealth, believes she has the right to enrage her son and to refuse him the joy of an honest marriage? She wouldn't give me any advance on my inheritance. And I, who pretend to be an avenger of injustices—I will look on her with tranquil eyes? No. I will not wrong my reputation, and on my oath, the good woman will learn to know men!

BETTY:

What astonishes me is that she knows men so little, for despite Miss Angelica's wonderful acting, Angelica isn't built like a man, and I perceive the difference very clearly.

MERLIN:

Oh, the devil! You are a connoisseur.

PHILLIP:

My poor Betty, take care that nothing can give my mother any suspicion of the truth.

BETTY:

Don't worry, but try to bring things to a conclusion soon; she might, in the end, perceive that the Count is a Countess.

PHILLIP:

She's right. It's time to act.

MERLIN:

Let's act, then. I agree to that. Go warn Angelica to meet us here. The Chevalier de Pharanambasse wishes to be paid. She knows what that means. As for you, wait for my instructions at the lawyers; I am going to bring the money myself. Goodbye. Soon the moment will come which will decide your destiny.

PHILLIP:

If you make me happy, I promise to share the money with you.

MERLIN:

Pretty words cost nothing.

PHILLIP:

These are not simple words. Hold on, Betty. I'm annoyed that I have only thirty shillings in my pockets, but buy some ribbons, I beg you.

BETTY:

This is a happy presage.

MERLIN:

Sir!

PHILLIP:

What is it?

MERLIN:

Don't you notice that I need a new hat?

PHILLIP:

I will have nothing that is not yours, on my oath.

(Exit Phillip)

MERLIN:

You will be well enough ribboned, it seems to me.

BETTY:

What a lovable little man is your master.

MERLIN:

You never found him so lovable before.

BETTY:

Me—I've always had an inclination for him. He needs to know all the trouble I've taken to put his mother in the frame of mind required for our little enterprise.

MERLIN:

And do you think that it will succeed? Let's talk seriously about that. Is she truly perfectly in love? Is she truly persuaded?

BETTY:

And would you prefer that she wouldn't do it? She is aging and very coquettish. A young man who appears to be, at least, very handsome and well-bred, desperately attaches himself to her—she'd be her own worst enemy if she didn't believe it.

MERLIN:

You're right.

BETTY:

He tells her she's young and pretty, and what could be easier than to convince her? She's happier than she's been for some time.

MERLIN:

And the mirror doesn't disturb her contentment a little?

BETTY:

God, mirrors! I believe she's got it in her head that taste has changed in looks, and the most wrinkled become the most fashionable.

MERLIN:

But, in fact, there are a thousand coquettes in London who don't wear others. Let's get down to business. Is she aware that the Count is dependent on an avaricious, quarrelsome, violent, imperious, asinine father? It was good to go that far.

BETTY:

Knowing that you impersonate this father. I have painted his portrait as nasty as possible.

MERLIN:

Very well, you have taught her to think this father has a daughter that he loves tenderly, and that he absolutely intends to see married before he will concern himself about the marriage of his son?

BETTY:

We talk of nothing else.

MERLIN:

Very well—that's the nub of the business. Has the Count adroitly insinuated to Madam that he needs money?

BETTY:

She is perfectly persuaded, but I warn you, the lady is a miser.

MERLIN:

No matter—she is in love, and I answer for the rest; all you have to do is be on the lookout, and second Tiggs and myself.

BETTY:

Here's Madam, and it would be better for her not to see you.

MERLIN:

That doesn't matter. On the contrary, I have a thrust to make at her.

(Enter Mrs. Hardwick)

MRS. HARDWICK:

Oh, my poor Betty, I am about to die of chagrin.

BETTY:

What is it, madam—what news?

MRS. HARDWICK:

I can't take it anymore. I am in despair. (seeing Merlin) Who is this fellow?

BETTY:

Him?

MRS. HARDWICK:

Who is he? What do you want? Who sent you here?

MERLIN:

My mistress sent me here, madam.

MRS. HARDWICK:

Who is your mistress?

MERLIN:

The Marquise. I have a letter for the Count.

MRS. HARDWICK:

A letter for the Count!

MERLIN:

Yes, madam. But I was just going to say to my mistress that I didn't find him, and that I merely had the honor of bowing to his grandmother.

MRS. HARDWICK:

What grandmother—grandmother, me, me, grandmother? Why look at this impudent creature—do I have the air of a grandmother?

BETTY:

One couldn't be more grossly mistaken.

MRS. HARDWICK:

It seems that everything that happens today is meant to drive me mad.

BETTY:

What has happened to you?

MRS. HARDWICK:

I have just seen the little Count in his carriage.

BETTY:

Well, madam?

MRS. HARDWICK:

My rascal of a son was with him.

BETTY:

What, madam—do they know each other?

MRS. HARDWICK:

I don't know, but Phillip knows that we love each other, and he'll have told the Count any number of lies about me.

BETTY:

Oh, madam, he has too much respect.

MRS. HARDWICK:

Him, respect! He's an unnatural creature who doesn't want me to marry.

BETTY:

The little fool.

MRS. HARDWICK:

He was deliberately wearing his brown wig, which makes him look at least thirty-five, to prevent me from appearing as young as I am.

BETTY:

He's got a bad spirit; he isn't yet twenty years of age.

MRS. HARDWICK:

Assuredly he isn't, and I had him so young, so young that it was a miracle I was able to do it.

BETTY:

And the little ingrate doesn't have any gratitude for that miracle.

MRS. HARDWICK:

I will be revenged on his ingratitude and I shall hurry to become a Countess.

BETTY:

You know how to take a better role.

MRS. HARDWICK:

What disturbs me is that this little Count is a good-looking man, and a good-looking man these days is rarely without many intrigues.

BETTY:

And if he has, madam, he ought to seem more lovable to you. In good faith, madam, would you accept a lover who has nothing to sacrifice to you?

MRS. HARDWICK:

No, but I don't want a husband who would sacrifice me to his mistress.

BETTY:

My word, madam, I can reply that I will put my hand in the fire that he'll never be unfaithful to you with a woman.

MRS. HARDWICK:

You see, they send him letters at my house.

BETTY:

That's not his fault.

MRS. HARDWICK:

I'd like to be sure of that.

BETTY:

Well, then, madam?

MRS. HARDWICK:

It's a clever person who takes time in advance to observe her situation.

TIFFANY:

(entering) Here's the fat lady who was with you for a long while yesterday.

MRS. HARDWICK:

That's the lady who comes to inform me of the news. Remain here, Betty, and if the Count comes, amuse him for a few moments.

(Exit Mrs. Hardwick and Tiffany)

BETTY:

Yes, on my oath this could turn out even more splendidly than Merlin himself imagines. This woman is suspicious: she's trying to discover some intrigues of our little Count, and she will discover that it isn't possible for him to have any— But, here he is.

(Enter Angelica dressed as the Count)

COUNT:

Oh, no, no, my child, tell your mistress she has nothing to fear. I have other affairs, I have other affairs, I tell you. I repeated this thirty times. Do me the pleasure of not troubling me any further.

BETTY:

You explain yourself cruelly, and you have, as I see, more good fortune than you expect.

COUNT:

Ah, the tiresome job of a handsome fellow, I can only appear happy. I have not a moment to myself—women of quality, bourgeois women, business women. One doesn't know which way to turn. There's a wife of a banker who persecutes me, and wherever I go, it rains messengers and letters from her.

BETTY:

These women have no class. Is it possible that such coolness on your part doesn't rebuke them or open their eyes? It amazes me that some cunning slut has not penetrated the real reason.

COUNT:

By God, I defy them all to guess it! I arrived here three months ago from the most backward province, but I've only begun to shine in the beau-monde in this disguise. I present to the most penetrating eyes this youthful, mannish air I have—the better to deceive them.

BETTY:

Yes, you imitate the manners of young men marvelously—it seems as if you had studied them all your life.

COUNT:

I copy them from one end to the other. I am confident of myself. The admiring looks I get from ladies of quality that I get for a "Zounds!" that costs me nothing. I brush off the prettiest creatures in the world with sang-froid. I am insolent with bureaucrats, honest and civil with soldiers. I desolate men of the cloth. I take tobacco gracefully enough, and am so perfect a young fellow I could be a drunk.

BETTY:

True, that's the sole accomplishment you lack. But all these perfections are not helpful, and do nothing to advance your affair. And Madam Hardwick is perhaps undeceived by now.

COUNT:

What?

BETTY:

She's put a spy on you who's giving her a report.

COUNT:

Oh, I know who that is— Her spy is one of us and she tells her nothing that Merlin hasn't dictated, and the pains she takes will only serve to better deceive her.

BETTY:

That's lucky. She's just seen you with Phillip.

COUNT:

We intended that.

BETTY:

Which means we are near the denouement.

COUNT:

I don't welcome it without a scrap. I wouldn't be happy without all the tricks we are using.

BETTY:

These good intentions are a wonderful thing. They excuse everything.

COUNT:

Merlin isn't going to come?

BETTY:

Apparently. You are perfect in all you must do.

COUNT:

I know my part by heart.

BETTY:

Think how to draw her out—I believe I hear Madam.

COUNT:

You didn't tell me she was at home. She might have heard us.

BETTY:

She might listen without having heard. The room is large and the good lady doesn't have a fine ear. But to be certain, hide for a minute, and let me converse with her quickly. Here she is, and she doesn't appear in good humor.

(The Count hides)

MRS. HARDWICK:

(entering) Well, Betty—hasn't he come?

BETTY:

No, Madam.

MRS. HARDWICK:

The rogue! He didn't send anyone.

BETTY:

No, Madam.

MRS. HARDWICK:

Little monster of perfidy!

BETTY:

Your anger is growing?

MRS. HARDWICK:

You know the terms we are on. I can see from his manners that he isn't on tenterhooks for me to marry him.

BETTY:

Well, Madam?

MRS. HARDWICK:

Well, Betty, he's in the same situation with a dozen others.

BETTY:

With a dozen others!

MRS. HARDWICK:

Among those others is a certain old Marquise, and they say he has strong engagements with her.

BETTY:

Better catch him in a hurry, Madam, or he will escape you. You've got no time to lose— Here he is.

MRS. HARDWICK:

Ah, my poor Betty, despite all they told me of him, I lack the strength to quarrel with him.

BETTY:

Poor lady.

(Enter Count)

COUNT:

Truly, Madam, I got mired in a fatiguing conversation this morning.

MRS. HARDWICK:

My nasty son was speaking with you. I had indeed foreseen it.

COUNT:

The most displeasing animal is an amorous old woman.

BETTY:

(to Mrs., Hardwick) What a nice compliment to make you.

MRS. HARDWICK:

They don't all seem frightful to you, sir, and a CERTAIN OLD MARQUISE among others.

COUNT:

Yes, Madam, precisely: she's a Marquise who bored me so—the old madwoman.

BETTY:

Wasn't she the one who sent to look for him here?

COUNT:

She herself, apparently.

BETTY:

I don't know exactly how old she is, but her valet takes all the world for grandmothers. Ask Madam.

MRS. HARDWICK:

Quiet, Betty, it's better for one not to know this sort of nonsense.

COUNT:

She's a woman who desolates me. She makes me lose reputation. Why, Madam, she tells the whole world I am in love with her, and that I am burning with impatience to be her husband.

MRS. HARDWICK:

It's true that the whole town speaks in the same manner.

COUNT:

The noise has gotten to you.

BETTY:

Truly, and much worse things have reached us.

COUNT:

What, Betty?

BETTY:

Madam has been informed that you are the hero of flirtations.

COUNT:

Me, the hero?—I am the Martyr! And despite all the feelings I have for you, I will be forced to leave you and take a rest in the country.

MRS. HARDWICK:

A rest in the country? What are you talking about?

COUNT:

I am overwhelmed by adventures—most of the young men are in the army, and all the coquettes are in London—and they're falling in my arms.

BETTY:

'Death, how mad they are! There are plenty of other men that know what to do with them. Aren't the bureaucrats just as good-looking as the soldiers? It seems to me that a young barrister in summer is better than an old Colonel in winter quarters.

COUNT:

You are right. But do women of the world reason that way? It's only the stars and caprice that govern what they do.

BETTY:

Which means that at present you are the object of stars and caprice.

MRS. HARDWICK:

No, Count, don't go, if you don't want to drive me to desperation.

COUNT:

Then tell me what you want me to do.

BETTY:

Eh! Why hesitate so? You love each other—why so much good manners? A good marriage according to the forms will cure Madam of her suspicions, and will give you protection from the persecutions you are suffering.

MRS. HARDWICK:

You say nothing in response to this, Milord Count?

COUNT:

I must wait until I know what you think.

MRS. HARDWICK:

Betty seems to me a good councilor.

BETTY:

Isn't it true?

COUNT:

But, Madam, at least let this business be extremely secret.

MRS. HARDWICK:

It will be, I have a lawyer who is discretion itself. Send to Mr. Goodspeed that I need him.

(Exit Betty)

MRS. HARDWICK:

I didn't know what to think, sir. You wish to take care of my rivals, while you wish to avoid attention.

COUNT:

I, Madam? I scorn them all. I've told you a hundred times about my father's bizarre humor. I fear a thousand obstacles on his part. Who knows whether he'll carry his caprice so far as not to permit our marriage—however advantageous to me it may be, if he doesn't find a considerable person to marry my sister. Take the trouble to believe he is entirely like that.

MRS. HARDWICK:

I love you a lot. I believe all that you tell me. I want to do whatever you wish. You wouldn't reap any glory from deceiving me.

(Enter Betty)

BETTY:

Sir there's a Mr. Barnabas asking for you.

COUNT:

Barnabas, you say, Barnabas?

BETTY:

Yes, Mr. Barnabas.

COUNT:

Strange man, Mr. Barnabas, who comes to visit me in your home.

MRS. HARDWICK:

You are the master, let him come— You know some oddly-named people, Count.

COUNT:

He's a gambler, a sort of card sharp, and that I admit to you with whom I foresaw I would have some uproar.

MRS. HARDWICK:

What sort of uproar? Be very careful. I can guess what it is. You owe him money.

COUNT:

Yes, Madam, a trifling 300 shillings, which he's already demanded of me with an innocence—

MRS. HARDWICK:

I really believe it. At his name alone I would wager he's a brute! Here he is! What a physiognomy.

MERLIN:

(entering, disguised) Hello, Madam—I am your valet.

COUNT:

(low to Betty) Ah, Betty, he's drunk. All is lost.

MERLIN:

I enter freely enough, as you see, but that's my manner, and at all times the Barnabases have always the same manner. Hello, drunkard, you're the one I'm after.

MRS. HARDWICK:

Have you come to have a debauch here?

MERLIN:

No, Madam, I've indeed dined, and my passion dominates. My custom is to pay serious visits after having had dinner.

COUNT:

Truly, Mr. Barnabas, you pick your time very ill.

MERLIN:

I pick my time ill, you say? By Jove, my dear, it seems to me that to settle the small accounts we have together, I couldn't do better than to meet you in this house.

BETTY:

(low to Count) He's getting to the point; don't lose control.

COUNT:

What's up? What do you mean? It seems that you take Madam for my treasurer?

MERLIN:

Why not? If she isn't yet, she will become so. Here's a most favorable opportunity, Madam; a little gentleman with such a fine air is worth doing something for.

COUNT:

He's drunk, Madam, as you see.

BETTY:

(to Count) His drunkenness makes good sense, let him alone.

MRS. HARDWICK:

I find him impertinent in all his manners.

COUNT:

I'm going to rough him up, and make him leave.

MRS. HARDWICK:

Rough him up. No—do nothing of the sort.

MERLIN:

What little chat are you all three having privately? You are speaking of me, on my oath.

COUNT:

We've got to rid ourselves of this drunk.

MERLIN:

Beautiful slip of a woman, by God, beautiful slip of a woman.

COUNT:

I wasn't prepared to see him in this condition.

BETTY:

Keep the bet, I tell you.

MERLIN:

I admire you from head to foot.

MRS. HARDWICK:

There's some good in his manners.

MERLIN:

Where does this cheat here unearth so many beauties? The Marquise is still brisk, very brisk.

COUNT:

He doesn't know what he's saying.

MERLIN:

On the subject of the Marquise—are you no longer interested in marrying her? So, it's all over? You've done well if you don't marry her—all the same, you'll have to make her reparations.

MRS. HARDWICK:

Oh, sir—reparations if he doesn't marry her. Explain yourself.

MERLIN:

They have some little accounts to settle.

MRS. HARDWICK:

I beg you—speak more plainly.

MERLIN:

He will cost you several thousand pounds—to get him out of the hands of this Marquise.

MRS. HARDWICK:

Make me understand this puzzle, Count.

COUNT:

I don't understand it myself.

MERLIN:

He is engaged, at least, this young man. But leave that. That isn't what brought me here. Let's talk of other things. Well, what is this three hundred pounds you owe me? Are you going to make me wait for it? Madam wants an account. Do you want to give me a bill drawn of some of your mistresses?

MRS. HARDWICK:

On some of his mistresses!

COUNT:

He's making a bad joke, Madam. If I lose my patience, just for a minute—

MERLIN:

I don't care. Let's get this over with, because I've got other business. Come, Madam, the money.

MRS. HARDWICK:

Why, truly, Mr. Barnabas is a highway robber.

MERLIN:

You might be more civil the way you express yourself, madam. Highway robber! Damn, I'm in your home!

COUNT:

Listen, Mr. Barnabas. You aren't in a condition to speak reasonably. If you continue to anger me, I will make you understand in a way—

MRS. HARDWICK:

Count, what are you going to do?

MERLIN:

The little chap is violent.

BETTY:

He'll strangle him in your room if you don't stop him.

MRS. HARDWICK:

Stop him—at least give him his 300 pounds—

MERLIN:

Give them to him, Madam? I would much prefer—

BETTY:

Hey, the little rogue, Madam—there's nothing else to do.

MERLIN:

No, if you please, Madam. I don't want to receive them from your hands. I don't intend for someone to say I am a thief. But the gentleman owes me 300 pounds. The truth is that if I don't have them immediately, one way or another—I esteem and respect you, Madam, I don't wish to set up a row in your house—but I will have the pleasure of killing him on your doorstep.

MRS. HARDWICK:

The pleasure of killing him—? Oh, just heavens.

MERLIN:

I laugh at all that—

MRS. HARDWICK:

Mr. Barnabas, I will find you your money.

COUNT:

No, Madam. Don't do it; I pray you.

BETTY:

Hurry, Madam. He's not the one to listen to, the little fanatic.

MRS. HARDWICK:

Count, come with me.

BETTY:

Hey, go, go, Madam. I will separate them if they try to fight.

MERLIN:

Us, fight! And why should we fight when Madam is arranging things?

MRS. HARDWICK:

You promise me to be good?

COUNT:

I will do what you wish, but I am doing myself a terrible violence in obeying you.

BETTY:

Little lion heart! Go quickly, Madam, go quickly.

(Exit Mrs. Hardwick)

MERLIN:

Is she gone?

BETTY:

Yes.

MERLIN:

Seems to me that for a drunk, I manage affairs pretty well.

COUNT:

And why did you affect this appearance? At first, you greatly worried me.

MERLIN:

Why, Madam, it's a little fancy I took in coming here. I have more than one role to play in this comedy, and the air and tone of a drunk perfectly disguise this face.

COUNT:

Where is Philip?

MERLIN:

Where you left him—at the attorney's. He's waiting for me and the 300 pounds.

BETTY:

Nothing can be done without that.

MERLIN:

No, no, child. No money, no attorney. It's the custom in London.

COUNT:

It's not beginning badly.

MERLIN:

The Marquise is waiting for Mr. Barnabas, who is going to take her place. We will be done with Mrs. Hardwick in a little while.

COUNT:

I worry something may interfere.

MERLIN:

Don't fret. I am practical and I know women. A young person loses a lover without too much pain because she has the hope of easily getting another. But for an older woman to let one go, he might never come back.

BETTY:

Pretty moral.

MERLIN:

It's very true. Consider.

BETTY:

Consider yourself and use sang-froid— Here's Madam.

(Enter Mrs. Hardwick)

MERLIN:

Yes, I am speaking naturally when I tell you this Mrs. Hardwick is better for you than the other—a brave lady, pretty, shapely, and young to boot, and who in things assuredly makes you see that— Ah, Madam, I beg your pardon. I was speaking freely to this young man, speaking my mind. I am without rancor. If someone owes me money, I ask for it. Once I am paid, I don't ask for it a second time.

MRS. HARDWICK:

There are 300 pounds in this purse, sir.

MERLIN:

Brand new, Madam.

MRS. HARDWICK:

Yes, truly.

COUNT:

Let's get this over with, my dear Mr. Barnabas; you are satisfied now. Your servant.

MERLIN:

Your valet. Goodbye, until we meet again. You are the most obliging person that I know.

(Barnabas leaves)

COUNT:

I am in despair over this adventure. And I am confused by the manner in which it terminated.

BETTY:

Good—confused! Do young men these days blush about such things? You must regard this 300 pounds as a sample of the wedding present Madam is giving you.

MRS. HARDWICK:

Has Mr. Goodspeed come?

BETTY:

One of the lackeys went to him. Do you want me to send another? I am as impatient as you are, and I wish it were signed and sealed already.

COUNT:

Betty is very much in my interests.

BETTY:

You're under no obligation. It's sympathy with Madam. I am frank, as you see.

(Enter Tiffany)

TIFFANY:

Sir, there's a lady in a golden carriage who asks for you.

MRS. HARDWICK:

A lady who asks for you?

BETTY:

We seem to be an address agency.

COUNT:

A lady who asks for me: what timing!

MRS. HARDWICK:

Just say the gentleman isn't here, simpleton.

TIFFANY:

Oh, damn, I didn't know you didn't want him to be here.

COUNT:

All sorts of misfortunes are happening to me.

BETTY:

Couldn't you find out what she wants?

COUNT:

Oh, that's not difficult. A big golden carriage— It's the Marquise.

MRS. HARDWICK:

The Marquise—

COUNT:

Yes, Madam.

TIFFANY:

She says that if you won't come down, don't give yourself any trouble—she will come up.

COUNT:

Poor Betty, you must go speak to her, I pray you.

BETTY:

What shall I say to her?

COUNT:

You will tell her— It's better that I go myself.

BETTY:

She will carry you off.

MRS. HARDWICK:

Remain here, Count.

COUNT:

Well then, Betty, you will say —

BETTY:

My word, tell her yourself. She's getting impatient. I believe she's coming herself.

COUNT:

It's she. What to do?

MRS. HARDWICK:

Hide.

(Enter Tiggs disguised as a Marquise.)

TIGGS:

My dear lady, your very humble servant. But for this gentleman who is always with you, as they say, I'd never pay you a superfluous visit like this.

BETTY:

Here's an honest Marquise.

COUNT:

Don't be offended, Madam, she's an extravagant.

MRS. HARDWICK:

I will have some trouble preventing myself from telling her off.

TIGGS:

Well, sir, are you finally finished, and will you come away. Your father and my nephew are waiting for us.

MRS. HARDWICK:

Truly, Madam, you play a strange role, running like this after a young man.

TIGGS:

What does that signify, Madam? Isn't he to be my husband?

MRS. HARDWICK:

Your husband him, your husband?

BETTY:

Good, it's starting very well.

MRS. HARDWICK:

Count, undeceive her, please.

COUNT:

Undeceive her! She is a madwoman. Haven't I told you so?

TIGGS:

Speak, sir, speak. What keeps you from speaking the truth naturally?

COUNT:

What use to tell her, Madam? Haven't I told you my thoughts a hundred times?

MRS. HARDWICK:

Truly, it must be strange to be surrounded by chimeras.

TIGGS:

What chimeras? You want me to call the Count a chimera?

BETTY:

If this conversation heats up, the Marquise's ears will be burning

TIGGS:

Speak, sir. Speak. Haven't I the word of your father?

COUNT:

I believe that he's given it to you.

MRS. HARDWICK:

What, sir?

COUNT:

That's why I advised you to keep it secret.

TIGGS:

Isn't your sister to marry my nephew?

COUNT:

It seems to me that I've heard it spoken of.

MRS. HARDWICK:

You never told me of it.

COUNT:

What good to bother you with such a trifle?

TIGGS:

Haven't I given my nephew most of my wealth in favor of this marriage?

COUNT:

That's a condition that my father exacted of you.

TIGGS:

Truly, he didn't exact it. I wanted to do it. You ought, after his death, to be the master of all his wealth. Isn't it right for him to seek to secure your sister's fortune?

COUNT:

My father has his views, Madam, and I have mine.

MRS. HARDWICK:

So everything she is true, Count?

TIGGS:

Yes, Madam, I am not a chimera, as you see.

MRS. HARDWICK:

Why make a mystery to me of all this?

COUNT:

Why bother you with it?— If you think I intend to sacrifice my feelings to my sister's interests—

TIGGS:

Oh—unnatural creature.

COUNT:

Am I not ready to disobey my father?

TIGGS:

Impious little creature.

COUNT:

And to give my oath to Madam: I'd sooner give myself up to death than to submit to marry her.

TIGGS:

Insolent! To say such a thing to my face!

BETTY:

That's what one calls a sacrifice according to form.

MRS. HARDWICK:

I am not charmed by his procedure.

COUNT:

May I not wish to love you alone in the world?

TIGGS:

Oh, there, there, little boy—your father will straighten you out—just wait.

COUNT:

My father is very reasonable, Madam, to force me to become the victim of a bullheadedness such as yours.

MRS. HARDWICK:

It's a horrible thing to persecute a child like this—you can see he doesn't love you.

TIGGS:

Oh, fie, fie, Madam, you ought to blush to entice him from me the way you are doing.

MRS. HARDWICK:

Entice him from you. What terms are you using, if you please!

TIGGS:

I use terms that agree with their subject.

MRS. HARDWICK:

I could indeed use the sole one there is to reply to this!

COUNT:

Ah, Madam.

BETTY:

Don't get carried away, Madam, or you, Count. You shall avenge yourself on her, and Madam will be punished enough by your not marrying her.

TIGGS:

I won't marry him, won't I? I've done with him. Read the contract, ingrate, read the contract. Money in hand, jewels, all my silverware. I've sacrificed everything to your mad expenses, and after all that I am going to suffer you to be in the arms of another woman!

COUNT:

Well, Madam, by what right do you force me to marry you against my will?

BETTY:

And if one married out of duty all the extravagants who made scenes like this, men would have a dozen wives.

TIGGS:

I have nobody here on my side. Your father will do something about your lies. I am going to bring him. You just wait! You just wait.

(Exit Tiggs)

BETTY:

Bring us your father, sir! What a reception. They say he's the strangest fellow in the world.

COUNT:

This is what I dread the most, I admit.

MRS. HARDWICK:

What shall we do?

COUNT:

I don't know where I am.

BETTY:

Nothing more embarrassing.

MRS. HARDWICK:

Can't you find some way?

COUNT:

Create, invent, my dear Betty.

BETTY:

Wait.

MRS. HARDWICK:

Have you some idea?

BETTY:

I'm rolling several little ideas around in my head. Give me a minute.

MRS. HARDWICK:

Tell us what it is quickly.

BETTY:

Tell me first, sir, is your father completely determined on this marriage?

COUNT:

Completely. Impossible to be more so. But solely because of my sister and this nephew who will marry her.

BETTY:

And because the fortune of the Marquise guarantees her nephew.

COUNT:

Exactly.

BETTY:

We will never change this father of yours.

MRS. HARDWICK:

Why not?

BETTY:

Because you have no nephew to marry his daughter. If your son were a child who would do things as you wish, you might still be able to work something out on that line— I believe your son is here. Chance brought him opportunely.

MRS. HARDWICK:

His visit bothers me more than the Marquise's.

(Enter Phillip)

PHILLIP:

There's a rumor about—which I don't find odd, and I am considering it. But what do I see? Here's the stepfather you are preparing for me.

COUNT:

Phillip, are you the son of Madam?

MRS. HARDWICK:

Don't let that surprise you; although he's full of strength, he's very young.

BETTY:

While Madam is his mother, she's just as young as her son.

PHILLIP:

Well, you chose well, Madam. Apparently— I have no complaint. The Count is a very great lord and you marry from interest.

MRS. HARDWICK:

So long as you are reasonable, I will do nothing to embarrass you.

PHILLIP:

I have reason to believe so, but the Marquise, Count, what will you say to her? You don't realize, mother, that this Marquise is a terrible woman who has large designs on the Count.

BETTY:

We don't know it? She just left. And your mother had great need of you in this business.

PHILLIP:

There's nothing I wouldn't do to oblige her.

MRS. HARDWICK:

The Marquise is a madwoman who doesn't know what she's saying.

BETTY:

But not counting the necessity, Madam, if he doesn't consent to marry the sister, the brother won't be yours, on my oath.

MRS. HARDWICK:

But at least it's not an indispensable necessity.

BETTY:

But not counting the necessity, Madam, by marrying him off in this way, you won't have the shame of little monkeys calling you grandma, and your son's children will only be your nephews and nieces.

MRS. HARDWICK:

You're right.

BETTY:

The meeting is really lucky. He must take the place of the nephew, I tell you.

COUNT:

The place of what nephew? What are you talking about?

BETTY:

Yes, the nephew of the Marquise. You must marry a very nice person who happens to be the sister of the Count.

PHILLIP:

The sister of the Count!

BETTY:

Do you know her?

PHILLIP:

Do I know her?

BETTY:

If you'd be so good as to agree quickly, your mother will give you part of her fortune, for, as her brother-in-law, you'd be reconciled with her.

PHILLIP:

To please you, Mom, I will do whatever you wish.

BETTY:

What a submission.

COUNT:

Ah, here's the Marquise with my father.

(Enter Tiggs as the Marquise, and Merlin as the father.)

MERLIN:

Well—what is it? Where is this young man? Damnation, Madam, let's not fight about it. Really, my son is to be married in half an hour.

MRS. HARDWICK:

How I prepare him for you, sir! I don't know what bad tales this Marquise has been telling you.

TIGGS:

I told you exactly that I would bring him here.

MRS. HARDWICK:

But I am not the cause of all the scorn your son feels for her.

TIGGS:

You see, sir, how they treat me.

MERLIN:

Scorn's got nothing to do with it, Madam. Let them scorn each other, let them detest each other, that frequently doesn't prevent marriage—people actually live together quite comfortably for all that. Come, little clown, prepare to do your duty.

COUNT:

Mercy, Father.

MERLIN:

You will marry her.

COUNT:

Don't force my inclinations.

MRS. HARDWICK:

I don't make him say that, you see.

MERLIN:

Madam, he will marry her or I am no longer his father.

MRS. HARDWICK:

Don't give up, Count.

MERLIN:

Now here's Mr. Goodspeed, my attorney. Come just as I sent for him.

BETTY:

Your attorney, sir. Mr. Goodspeed. He is indeed an attorney. The matter's going well. It isn't difficult.

MERLIN:

Don't worry, all will go well.

(Enter Goodspeed)

GOODSPEED:

Good day to all the honorable company.

MERLIN:

Come in, Mr. Goodspeed, come in.

MRS. HARDWICK:

Why, sir, what do you intend to do?

GOODSPEED:

I was passing by here, Sir. By chance, I have your contracts with me—with the names left blank, and I saw you enter, so—

MERLIN:

With your permission, Madam, we will not delay filling those names in.

MRS. HARDWICK:

But, sir—you dare to conclude contracts in my house. I don't understand anything of your ways.

MERLIN:

It can be done in a minute.

MRS. HARDWICK:

Mr. Goodspeed, I shall tear up your papers.

COUNT:

Let him do it, Madam. He cannot make me sign against my wishes.

MERLIN:

Listen to this. Here's a little cheat who's very rebellious.

TIGGS:

Does it astonish you? It's Madam who corrupts him.

COUNT:

Look, Father, be just to yourself and to me. Question the Marquise. I beg her pardon for speaking this way before her, but she has forced me to do it. Look at her airs and her manners—compare them without prejudice to Madam's charms.

MRS. HARDWICK:

Without vanity, there's quite a difference.

MERLIN:

Yes, The Marquise has a face which is a bit lumpish—it seems to me.

COUNT:

You gave me life; don't make it unlivable.

MERLIN:

He's weakening me,

BETTY:

Courage, sir.

COUNT:

And don't constrain me to spend my life with a person I cannot abide.

MRS. HARDWICK:

How nicely put.

MERLIN:

Yes, truly, he explains himself clearly. (To Tiggs) What have you to say?

TIGGS:

All I can say is that it doesn't surprise me. You promised him to me—I intend to have him. Or your daughter will have neither my fortune, nor my nephew.

MERLIN:

Ah, you've got it, Madam. You shall have him, Come, come, Mr. Goodspeed. I have given my word and it's sacred. So write!

MRS. HARDWICK:

He will have to write it in the street.

COUNT:

Well, if marrying my sister is a thing about which you are so sensitive, our meeting here is marvelous luck.

MERLIN:

What?

COUNT:

My sister tenderly loves the son of Madam Hardwick, you see.

MERLIN:

My daughter loves your son?

COUNT:

Yes, father, and he is crazy about her.

MERLIN:

Listen to that. But here's a sudden romance I've heard nothing of.

MRS. HARDWICK:

Neither did I, to say the truth,

COUNT:

It's been a while since I opened my heart to you about it, but you wouldn't listen to me.

MRS. HARDWICK:

What! It was she—

PHILLIP:

She herself. We spoke about it a hundred times, the Count and I, without knowing each other's position. Because I was ignorant of how things stood between you two.

MERLIN:

It doesn't surprise me that you've met them together so often.

MRS. HARDWICK:

But, truly, this is very wonderful.

MERLIN:

Sometimes, events speak for themselves, Marquise.

TIGGS:

These are only stories. Let Madam do for her son what I am ready to do for my nephew. I am giving him 6,000 pounds in favor of his marriage.

BETTY:

Six thousand pounds!

COUNT:

If ever you were charitable, Madam, it is time to declare yourself now.

MERLIN:

Come—six thousand pounds to this young fellow.

MRS. HARDWICK:

And I, I give ten thousand pounds to my son.

PHILLIP:

How much I have to thank you for.

MERLIN:

Ten thousand pounds—going once, going twice—

PHILLIP:

Come, Mr. Goodspeed, fill in my mother's name and ten thousand pounds.

TIGGS:

Twelve thousand.

MERLIN:

What, Mr. Goodspeed? Here's a bid. Well, madam?

TIGGS:

Well, I have two thousand pounds of jewels I can add in; I will give it to your daughter.

BETTY:

Come, courage, Madam—don't lose a bargain for such trifles.

MERLIN:

So, fourteen thousand.

MRS. HARDWICK:

I have only 40,000 pounds. I'll give half.

MERLIN:

Twenty thousand pounds—once, twice—gone for twenty thousand pounds. Write, Mr. Goodspeed, write to the highest bidder. (to Marquise) Would you care to offer something more?

TIGGS:

So, sir, this is the way you keep your promise to me!

MERLIN:

What do you want me to do, Madam? I gave you my word. But you know that one's word is the slave of one's interest.

TIGGS:

You are not yet where you think. I will have him, dead or alive, and my nephew is not a man who will suffer his aunt to be insulted like this.

(She rushes out)

PHILLIP:

She's in quite a rage.

BETTY:

(to Mrs. Hardwick) You are mistress of the battlefield.

MERLIN:

You see I can be persuaded by merit.

MRS. HARDWICK:

I have only done this for you, Count.

COUNT:

I want nothing of Phillip's, I assure you.

GOODSPEED:

Nothing to do but sign.

MRS. HARDWICK:

Let's sir.

GOODSPEED:

No, Madam, you sign first. Gentlemen after ladies.

MERLIN:

Yes, Madam, that's the rule.

MRS. HARDWICK:

You know things better than I— (signing)

MERLIN:

This has given me a bit of trouble. Well, sir, it's in order?

COUNT:

Now it's only a question of—

MERLIN:

I understand you. The account accompanying you to your office. Make your sister sign and bring her here.

MRS. HARDWICK:

It would be better if we went together.

MERLIN:

Together, Madam, no, if you don't mind. There are certain are certain proprieties about meetings that it is wise to observe. I am strict as the devil about such proprieties.

BETTY:

Have you ever heard tell of a man more bizarre and more capricious! Let him do it his way for fear he'll change his mind.

MRS. HARDWICK:

He's better do as you suggest. But don't be slow, Count.

COUNT:

I'll return momentarily.

(Exit Count)

MERLIN:

Here's an odd little business that turned out well.

BETTY:

He's only done as we told him.

MERLIN:

You've never seen his sister?

MRS. HARDWICK:

No, never.

MERLIN:

She is a little charmer. They resemble each other like two drops of water. Isn't that true?

PHILLIP:

The most adorable person in the world. I don't know how to tell you, sir—

MERLIN:

The most pretty nature, you will be charmed to have a sister-in-law like that— Because it's not necessary to call her your daughter-in-law.

MRS. HARDWICK:

No, truly.

MERLIN:

And I don't want her to call you mother-in-law.

BETTY:

It would be ridiculous.

MERLIN:

Sister-in-law is somewhat more pleasing to the ear.

MRS. HARDWICK:

It appears to me that way, too.

MERLIN:

There's something more serious in the other.

(Enter Jackson)

MERLIN:

It's my page, Madam. Here he is quite out of breath.

JACKSON:

Ah, sir.

MERLIN:

What's wrong with you?

JACKSON:

The Marquise—

MERLIN:

What's she done?

MERLIN:

She has eloped with the Count!

MRS. HARDWICK:

Eloped with my husband!

BETTY:

The effrontery to elope with a man.

JACKSON:

She's got the devil in her. She also carried off the attorney. She watched for them to leave here.

MERLIN:

The Marquise has carried off my child! She will marry him.

MRS. HARDWICK:

What, sir—she will marry him?

MERLIN:

Would you marry him after such an affront?

MRS. HARDWICK:

It's no dishonor for a young man. You must act quickly.

MERLIN:

Useless, Madam. The Marquise is a strange woman, and I fear we will never have news of her or my son again.

MRS. HARDWICK:

Ah, good heavens—what are you saying?

MERLIN:

And I am so despairing myself, that I believe, no one will ever speak of me as a father again.

MRS. HARDWICK:

I will die of shame! Don't leave me, Betty. I am going to tell the whole world about this.

(Exit Mrs. Hardwick and Betty)

PHILLIP:

How I fear her anger when she learns the truth.

MERLIN:

She'll have to be patient. Think only of your happiness. You will possess Angelica, you ought to be content. (turning to the Audience) I hope with all my heart that the company is, too.

(he bows deeply)

CURTAIN

ABOUT THE TRANSLATOR

Frank J. Morlock has written and translated many plays since retiring from the legal profession in 1992. His translations have also appeared on Project Gutenberg, the Alexandre Dumas Père web page, Literature in the Age of Napoléon, Infinite Artistries.com, and Munsey's (formerly Blackmask). In 2006 he received an award from the North American Jules Verne Society for his translations of Verne's plays. He lives and works in México.

www.ingramcontent.com/pod-product-compliance
Lightning Source LLC
LaVergne TN
LVHW040116080426
835507LV00039B/381